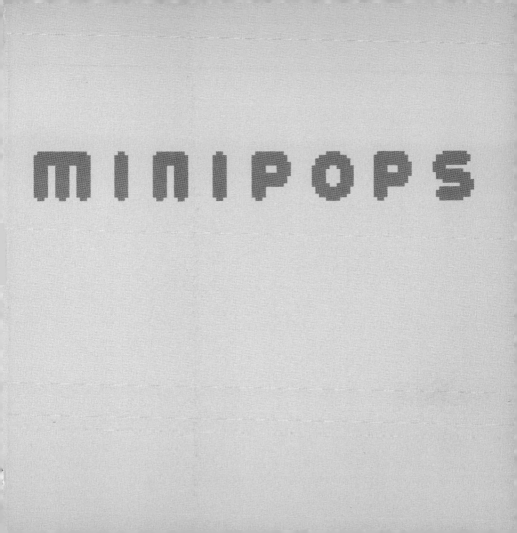

This book is dedicated to the memory of my grandparents: George Robinson. The finest pipe-smokin', bus–drivin', cartoon-lovin' man in Lincolnshire. Cris Robinson. A super woman who still loved pop music well into her seventies, made the best apple crumble, and taught me that the buttons on a video recorder are named incorrectly: it shouldn't be "rewind" or "fast forward"; it's "push it back" or "push it forward".

Minipops
Craig Robinson

First published in 2004 by Mitchell Beazley,
an imprint of Octopus Publishing Group Ltd,
2–4 Heron Quays, London E14 4JP

ISBN 1 8453 302 93

To order this book as a gift or an incentive contact
Mitchell Beazley on 020 7531 8481

A CIP catalogue copy of this book is available
from the British Library

Commissioning Editor **Hannah Barnes-Murphy**
Executive Art Editor **Auberon Hedgecoe**
Production **Seyhan Esen**

Set in Gill Sans

Printed and bound in Hong Kong

MINIPOPS

Craig Robinson

MITCHELL BEAZLEY

There was a evening in The Devonshire Arms pub in London during the summer of 1999 where a friend of mine, Delme, gave me the first encouraging comment on these new figures I'd drawn that I called Minipops. Sadly, I don't remember the exact words, but it was along the lines of, "there's life in them Minipops!" Thankfully, the book that you are holding kind of proves him right; and I'm exceedingly happy about that.

Minipops sound dull when you try and explain them ("they're small drawings of popstars; about 25 pixels high"); but somehow they seem to have caught peoples' attention.

Making them has been a joy, a challenge, infuriating, hard work, and a lesson. It's made my website – flipflopflyin.com – more popular than I could possibly have imagined. I owe Minipops a lot. I hope you enjoy flicking through the following pages and trying to guess who you're looking at (you can turn to the back for the answers); and if this book is a present: Happy Birthday or Merry Christmas!

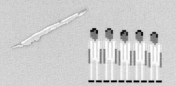

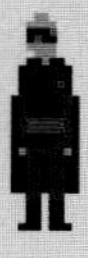
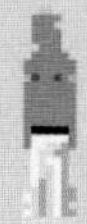
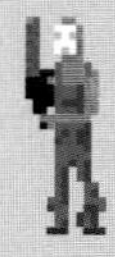

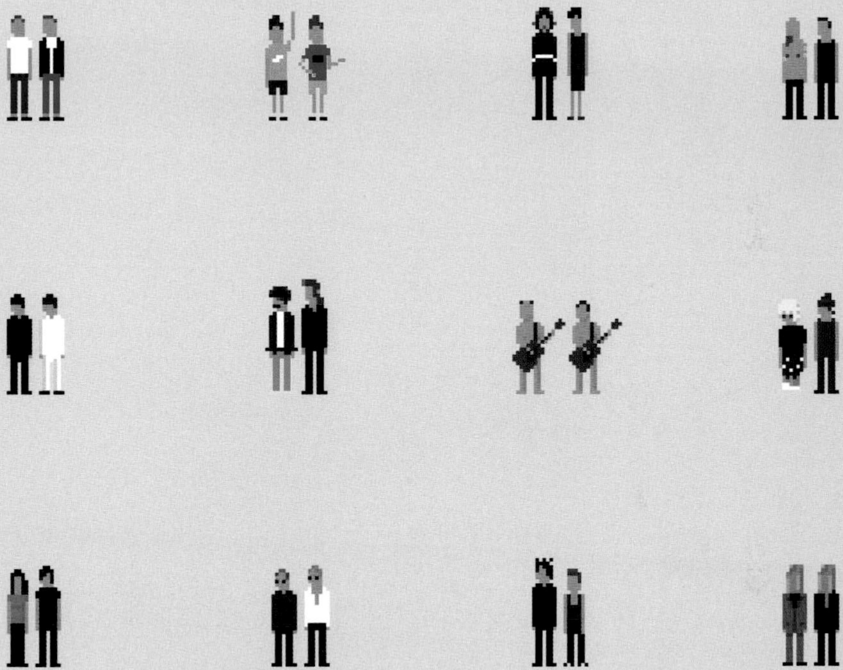

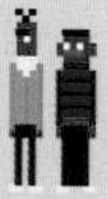
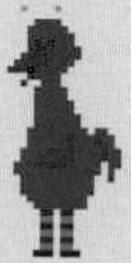
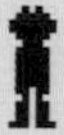
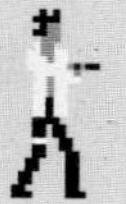
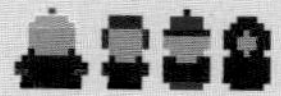
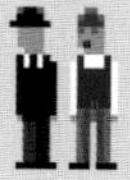
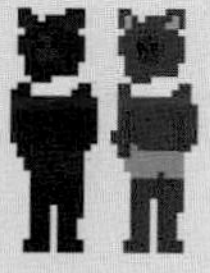

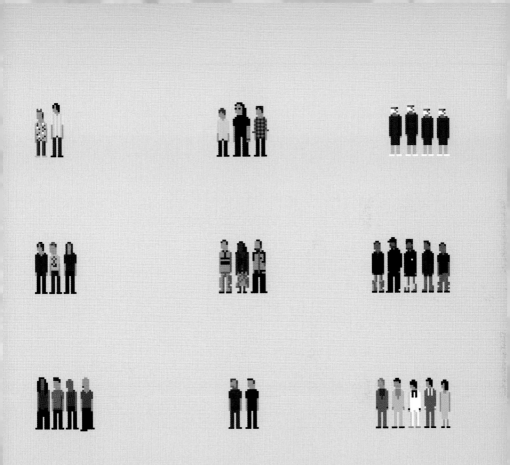

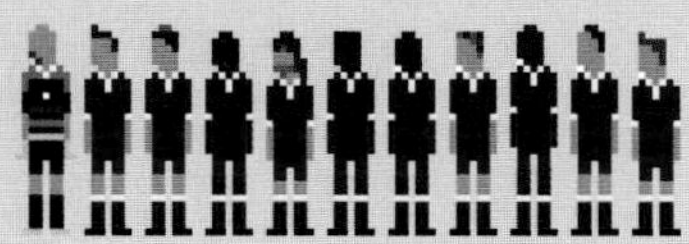

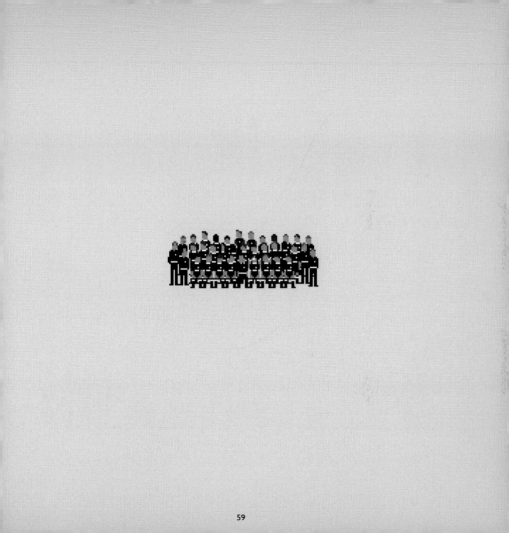

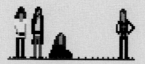

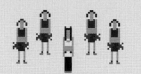

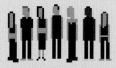

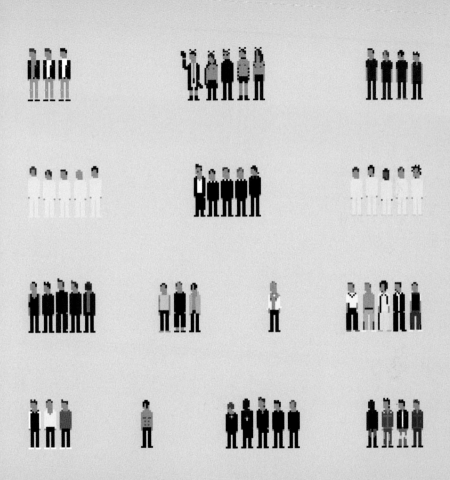

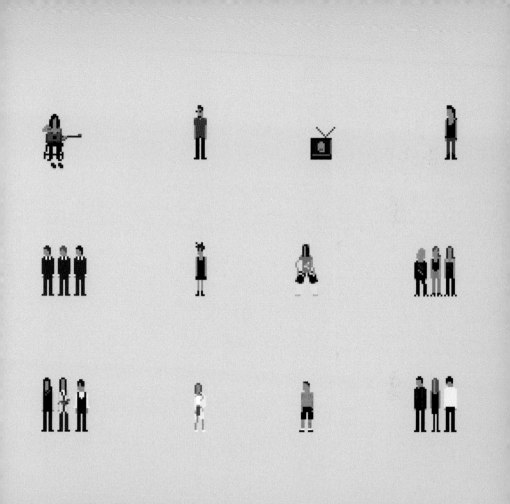

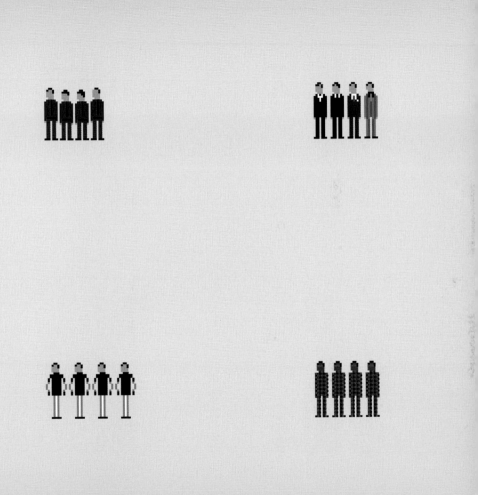

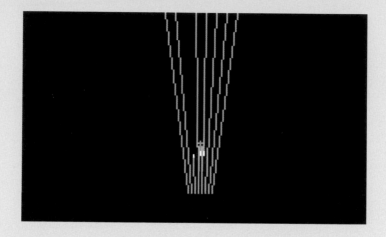

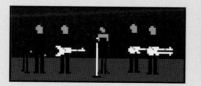
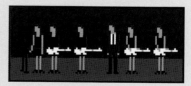

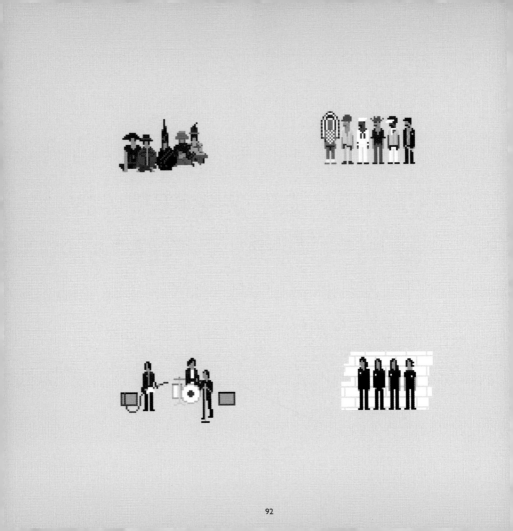

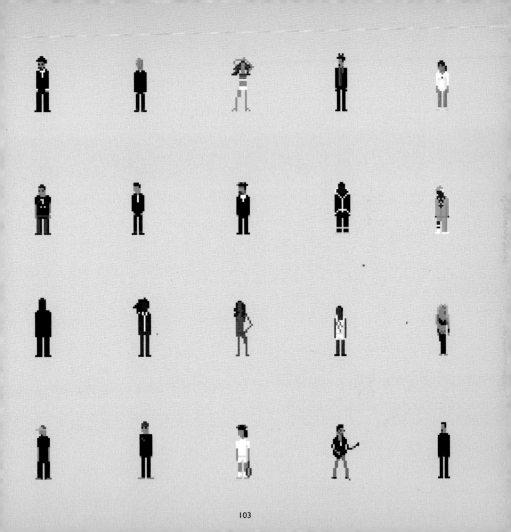

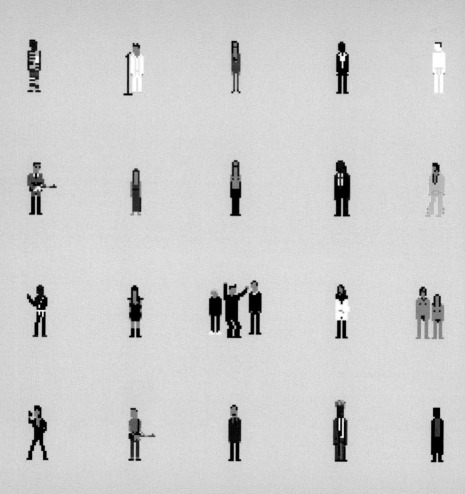

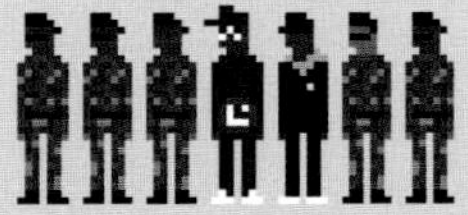

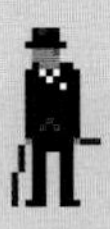

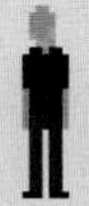

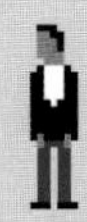

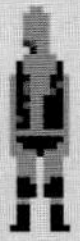

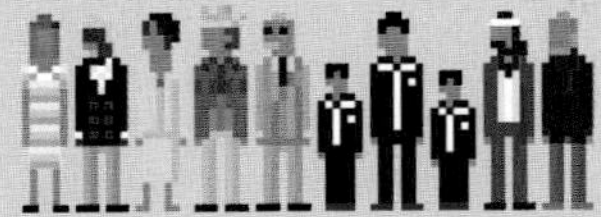

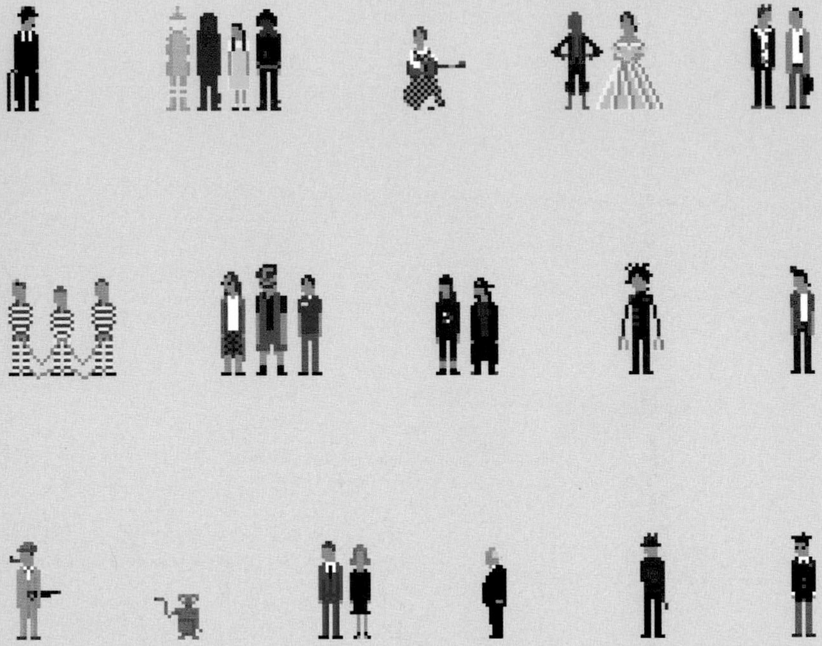

If any of those are real melon-scratchers, here's a list of them so you can sleep tonight:

Page 7: **Adam & Eve**

Page 8: **The Beach Boys** (this was the first Minipop I ever made. It was a Sunday night, nothing on telly, so the computer got switched on and I began drawing my favourite group as small as possible, but still recognizable. That lack of interesting programmes on TV lead to you holding this book – viva British TV!)

Page 9: **Flaming Lips**; **George Formby**; **U2** around the time of *All That You Can't Leave Behind*; **Rolling Stones**; **Audrey Hepburn** as Holly Golightly in *Breakfast At Tiffany's*; **The Darkness**; **Bonnie Prince Billy** (looking gorgeous, as ever. Lent his name to my lovely cocker spaniel); **Tatu**; **Barry White**; **Badly Drawn Boy** (badly drawn Badly Drawn Boy?); **The Strokes**; **The Libertines**; **Kings Of Leon**; **Shakin' Stevens** (when I was about 9 years old, I went to a wedding with my family. Not much of a dancer, my Mum had to bribe me with the offer of buying me an Adam & The Ants album if I danced with her. I danced to Green Door by Shaky, and a few days later, collected a brand spanking new album); **Daft Punk**

Page 10: **Eminem**: in the Without Me video; as he kinda normally looks; and trying to be scary with a chainsaw, grrr!

Page 11: **The Police**; **Soft Cell**; **The B-52's**; **Milli Vanilli** (I feel sorry for those two blokes. After all this Pop Idol stuff, I can't help feeling that they were hard done by, now that having virtually no talent is seen as a good thing); **The Human League** (a band that will always remind me of my pre-teen years, sat in the dining room at home, doing my homework whilst my dad, an architect, would sit at his drawing board doing complex plans of various buildings. He was the one who bought their *Dare* album, and very glad I am about that); **Culture Club**; **Curiosity Killed The Cat** (a posh London band who released a few decent singles in the eighties. Most famous, I guess, for their singer's long un-remember-able name – Ben Volpeliere-Pierrot – and his backwards fisherman's cap and puppet-style dancing. Somehow managed to get Andy Warhol to imitate Bob Dylan in their Misfit video); **ABC**; **Billy Idol**

Page 12: **Adam and the Ants** (the best band in the world ever ever ever and no one will ever ever ever be better. That's what I would have said when I was 12 years old. Although my opinion has changed a bit since then, they're still up there); **Roxy Music**; **Sigue Sigue Sputnik**; **Madness** (their Baggy Trousers 7" single was the first record I ever bought. I wrote my name on the back of it, and filled in the "O"s so they look like eyes)

Page 13: **Clint Eastwood** as The Man With No Name in Sergio Leone's spaghetti westerns; **LL Cool J** (which, as you all know, stands for Ladies Love Cool James. I have a friend called James, and as luck would have it, he's cool and ladies love him); **Hercule Poirot**; **Crocodile Dundee**; **Chopper**; **Bo Diddley**; **Karl Marx**; **Sherlock Holmes**; **Wesley Willis** (Rock over London, rock on Chicago!); **Woody Allen**; **Cat Stevens**; **Osama Bin Laden**; **The Incredible Hulk**; **Long John Silver**; **Demis Roussos** (my Mum liked him); **Joan Of Arc**; **Richard Branson**; **Kylie Minogue** (aaah, Kylie…); **Robert Johnson** (I had to guess at the colour of his clothes here, 'cos the only photos of him are black and white); **Indiana Jones** (without the Temple Of Doom, thankfully)

Page 14: *Star Wars*: **Luke Skywalker**; **Princess Leia**; **Lando Carlissian**; **Obi Wan Kenobi**; **Darth Vader**; **Yoda**; **Han Solo**; **Chewbacca**; **Boba Fett**; **C3PO**; **R2D2**

Page 15: **Fawlty Towers**; **Morecambe & Wise**; **Cilla Black**; *Minder*; **Vic Reeves and Bob Mortimer in** *Catterick*; *Father Ted*; **Chris Moyles**; *Blockbusters*; **Rod Hull and Emu** (for readers outside the UK, these are all British TV things. *Fawlty Towers* is the best sitcom ever; Morecambe & Wise were superb comedians, whose Christmas specials were fantastic; Cilla Black is a former singer and TV celeb; *Minder* was a show about a dodgy dealing fellow and his "minder"; Vic and Bob are comedians who've been around for a while now, *Catterick* being their latest show; *Father Ted* was a series about three priests living on an island in Ireland; Chris Moyles is a radio DJ; *Blockbusters* was a game show for students; and Rod Hull and Emu, well, he was a wiry-haired fellow with his arm inside an emu puppet who was a bit mental. Rod Hull sadly died when he fell of his roof trying to fix the TV aerial)

Page 16: **My Bloody Valentine**; **Scissor Sisters**; **Busted**; **The Beta Band**; **The Datsuns**; **The Vines**; **R.E.M.**; **The Donnas**; **Interpol**; **Manic Street Preachers** – with and without Richey Edwards; **Prodigy**

Page 17: **Prince**; **Diego Maradona** (the first time I remember saying the f-word in front of my mother was during the England v Argentina match in the 1986 World Cup. I don't need to explain at what point during that game I said that word, do I?); **Elvis Presley** wearing his gold lamé suit (which, I recently read, he only ever wore once. Well, well, well…)

Page 18–19: **The Beatles** in sharp grey suits; *HELP!*; *Abbey Road* (my favourite Beatles album); *Yellow Submarine*; and as Sgt. Pepper's Lonely Hearts Club Band

Page 20: **Sex Pistols**; **U2** around the time of *The Joshua Tree*; **The Monkees**; **Garbage**; **N*E*R*D**; **Happy Mondays**; **Arab Strap**; **Badly Drawn Boy** (this was done in the early days before he wore the hat all the time); **New Order** (one of my favourite bands. It was difficult to choose the clothes to draw, 'cos there's none that are particularly recognizable; so I just went for what they were wearing when they played live at the Reading Festival in 1998, which was one of the best concerts I've ever seen); **Frank Zappa**; **UNKLE**; **Black Lace**; **Altern 8** (Nice one! Top one! Get sorted!); **T Rex**; **The KLF**; **The Chemical Brothers**

Page 21: **Batman**; **Superman**; **Spiderman**

Page 22: **The Art Guys**; *The Breakfast Club* (although this was one of my favourite films when I was a teenager, and I still have a bit of a crush on Molly Ringwald, I never did understand the bit where Emilio Estevez screams and the window smashes. How does that happen? I've tried it, and the window doesn't even wobble); **CHiPs**; *The Blues Brothers*; **David Hasselhoff** as Michael Knight in *Knightrider* and Mitch Buchanan in *Baywatch*; **The Goodies**; *Diff'rent Strokes*; **Cheech and Chong**

Page 23: **Hugh Hefner with some of his lovely Playmates** (any man who spends his life in pyjamas has gotta be someone to admire)

Page 24: **John Lee Hooker**; **Peter Green**; **Steven Van Zandt** (at times his name is augmented with the words "Miami" or "Little" at the start. Most of you will know him as one of the actors in *The Sopranos*, but for me, he'll always be Bruce Springsteen's guitarist); **Roy Orbison**

Page 25: *Buena Vista Social Club*; **Phil Spector's** *A Christmas Gift For You* (the only album you need at Christmas time. In fact, it's not just good for Christmas, it's good all year round)

Page 26: **Travis Bickle** (*Taxi Driver*); **Spartacus**; **Starsky & Hutch**; *The Graduate*; **Michael Myers** (*Halloween*); *Sex and The City*; **Magnum PI**; **The Blue Man Group**; **Michael Moore**

Page 27: **Columbo** (my TV detective of choice)

Page 28: **Pavement**; **James**; **Kenickie**; **Sonic Youth**; **Lo Fidelity Allstars**; **Bis**; **The Primitives**; **These Animal Men** (I could tell you a story here, but I'd embarrass my friend Helen greatly, so I won't); **Morphine**

Page 29: **Julian Cope** hiding inside a tortoise shell; **Jilly Cooper**; **Andy Warhol**; **Liam Lynch**; **Lord Nelson**; **Michael Jordan**; **Sun Ra**; **Trent Reznor**; **Keith Harris and Orville**; **Norah Jones**; **Grace Jones**; *Braveheart*; **Kate Bush**; **Bagpuss**; **Alizee** (everyone's favourite French teenage nymph); **Gillian Welch**; **Will Smith** (in *Men In Black*); **Rufus Wainwright** (if I ever get married, and if this book sells enough for me to be as rich as Elton John, I would hire Rufus to play at the wedding reception); a **Space Invader**; **Pharrell Williams**

Page 30: **Stereophonics**; **Ween**; **Primal Scream**; **The Posies**; **Weezer**; **Pixies**; **Royal Trux**; **Salaryman**; **Blink 182** (I know; their name isn't spelled with a capital letter at the start, but I can't stand this e.e. cummings rubbish)

Page 31: **The Wonder Stuff**; **Simple Minds**; **Idlewild**; **Radiohead**; **Big Country**; **Smashing Pumpkins**; **Marion**; **Super Furry Animals** (the best British band around these days, I reckon. Why they're not superstars, I'll never know); **Live**

Page 32: **The Two Ronnies**; **Tom Baker** as Doctor Who; a **Dalek**; **Sir Jimmy Saville**; *Dad's Army*; **The Krankies**; *The Office*; *Only Fools and Horses*; **Richard O'Brien** (in The Crystal Maze)

Page 33: **Felicity Shagwell**; **Austin Powers**; **Dr Evil** and **Mini Me**

Page 34: The Stock Aitken Waterman page: **Mel and Kim**; **Dead Or Alive**; **Rick Astley**; **Hazell Dean**; **Bananarama**; **Sinitta**; **Big Fun**; **Divine**; **Stock Aitken Waterman** (at the time, in the eighties, S/A/W were kinda seen as the devil's record producers in the UK; but I'd rather have them back than all this *Pop Idol* stuff, anyday. Plus, you can't argue with some of the songs they've had a hand or two in: You Spin Me Round (Like A Record), I Should Be So Lucky, Respectable, You Think You're A Man, Love In The First Degree)

Page 35: **Erasure**; **Beavis and Butthead**; **Everything But The Girl**; **Queens of the Stone Age**; **The Webb Brothers**; **Hall and Oates** (oddly, I just downloaded I Can't Go For That, I forgot how good it was. This, by the way, is one of my favourite Minipops); **Tenacious D**; **Moldy Peaches**; **Fiery Furnaces**; **Whitehouse**; **Roxette**; **2 Many DJs** (from Belgium, one of my favourite places in the world)

Page 36: **Vanilla Ice**; **Bootsy Collins**; **Macy Gray**; **Seal**

Page 37: **Gonzales**; **Peaches**; **Lady Godiva**; **Beth Orton**

Page 38: **Massive Attack's glass fellow** off the cover of their *100th Window* album; **Takako Minekawa**; *Withnail & I*; **Emmylou Harris**; **Dick Whittington**; **Pee Wee Herman**; **Pope John Paul II**; **Sisters of Mercy**; **RZA** as

Bobby Digital; **Elton John**; **Gary Glitter**; **Andre the Giant** (although he doesn't look that giant next to Gary Glitter, which is a bit of an error, for which I apologize); **Haysi Fantayzee**; **Justin Timberlake**; **Miss Kittin**; **David Byrne** in the big suit he wore in the Talking Heads film *Stop Making Sense* (but still, the suit doesn't look as big as it should do. Sorry again); **Elliot Smith**; **Chas & Dave**; a **Money Mark doll** (at the time, Mo Wax was a pretty hip record label. Money Mark was one of their artists. He was quite good. And they made some dolls of him. I decided to do a Minipop of the doll instead of the man himself. Not sure why); **Alice In Wonderland** (if you've not done it already, you should read the book and rid your brain of the Disney-ized version)

Page 39: **Massive Attack**; **Abba**; **Sparks**; **Cuban Boys** (I must admit, I have absolutely no idea who this band is); **The Mamas and the Papas**; **Tori Amos**; **The Make-up**; **Ray Charles**; **Fleetwood Mac**

Page 40: Sesame Street (**Bert & Ernie**, **Big Bird**, and **Elmo**); **Sid Vicious**; *South Park*; **Mr Benn** and **the Shopkeeper**; **Aphex Twin** × 3 (the big bears he had with him at one point; the man himself; and the man himself with the body of a lady in the Windowlicker video)

Page 41: **Devo** (Q: Are we not Men? A: We are Minipops!); **Duran Duran**; **Japan**; **A Flock Of Seagulls**; **Kajagoogoo**; **Transvision Vamp**; **Blondie**; **Thompson Twins**; **Queen** (in the Radio Ga Ga video)

Page 42: **Willie Nelson**; **Hank Williams**; **The Flying Burrito Brothers**; **Johnny Cash** (I'm sad to say that there's not enough country artists as Minipops. I'm not sure why I've not done more. Maybe I should. Maybe the next book should be a Nashville Minipops special…)

Page 43: **The White Stripes**

Page 44: **Mötley Crüe**; **Pamela Anderson**; **Kid Rock**

Page 45: **Bent**; Yo La Tengo; **Clinic**; **Ben Folds Five**; **Morcheeba**; **Asian Dub Foundation**; **Skunk Anansie**; **Lemon Jelly**; **Soulwax**

Page 46: **Jerry Springer**; **Blackadder**; *Dawson's Creek*; *A Clockwork Orange*; *Thunderbirds*; *Miami Vice*; *Friends*; **Ant & Dec** (Brit TV presenters); **Rupert The Bear**

Page 47: **Madonna** × 3: nude hitchhiking in Sex; Music; in the video for that James Bond song

Page 48: **Windsor Davies** and **Don Estelle** (from *It Ain't Half Hot, Mum*, a Brit telly show); **Robin Hood**; **Merlin**; **The Lincoln Imp** (my home town is also this little fellow's home town. Lincoln, it should be noted, is a small but nice city. It's worth a visit to see the cathedral which is magnificent, and it's where this little fellow lives. One day in the 14th century, Satan sent two of his imps out to do their dirty work. One of them was quite brave and started hassling an angel. The angel in return, turned the imp to stone. And he's still there today.)

Page 49: **Ultramagnetic MCs**; **Janet Jackson** and **Justin Timberlake** at the Superbowl creating a huge fuss about nothing; **Janet Jackson** again, but with some bloke's arms covering her bosoms this time; **Kelis**; **Wu Tang Clan**; **Suge**

Knight; **Ol' Dirty Bastard**; **Beastie Boys**; **Ice T** and friend with gun; **Lil' Kim**; **the Streets**; **Run DMC**

Page 50: **Harry Nilsson** (forget Without You; and go straight to *The Point*, a wonderful album, with some of the most gorgeous melodies ever written); **Morrissey**; **Jerry St Clair** (*Phoenix Nights*); **Joan Jett**; **Van Dyke Parks** (buy *Song Cycle*. Go on, do it now! You won't regret it); **David Holmes**; **Cornelius**; **James Brown**; **Q Tip**; **the dog out of Daft Punk's Da Funk video**; **Judge Jules**; **Richard Ashcroft**; **Tim 'Love' Lee**; **Beethoven**; **Bruce Lee**

Page 51: **Les Rhythmes Digitales**; **Coldcut**; **Steely Dan**; **the burning chap off the cover of Pink Floyd's *Wish You Were Here***; **Air**; **Nancy Sinatra** and **Lee Hazlewood**; *Wayne's World*; **Lamb**; *The X-Files*

Page 52: **Karl Lagerfeld**; **Keith Haring**; **Mario Testino**; **Hiromix**; **Hedi Slimane**; **Vincent Gallo**; **Winney**; **Alexander McQueen**; **Yves Saint Laurent**; **Alek Wek**; **Jeremy Scott**; **Naomi Campbell**; **Chloë Sevigny**; **Tom Ford**; **Milla Jovovich**; **Steven Meisel**; **Donatella Versace**; **Marc Jacobs**; **Sofia Coppola**; **Harmony Korine** (this whole page is full of Minipops that I did for a website that I made for a very cool shop called Colette in Paris. I, you need to know, am one of the least cool people I know. My dress sense is virtually laughable. I really do try and avoid clothes shops as much as is possible. As I write these words, I'm wearing a t-shirt I bought in 1997, and now it has so many holes it looks more like a doily than a t-shirt. The point of telling you all about my clothes is that a lot of these Minipops are of the fashion world, therefore I know nothing about them. And I'm not sure why Jeremy Scott's got a blue bit on his head, but there you go)

Page 53: **Kate Moss**

Page 54: **They Might Be Giants**; **Rage Against The Machine**; **The Doors**; **Oasis**; **Ramones**; **Suicide**; **The Who**; **Siouxsie and the Banshees**; **The Bee Gees**

Page 55: **ZZ Top**; **Def Leppard**; **Led Zeppelin**; **Kiss**; **Cheap Trick**; **AC/DC**; **Megadeth**; **Aerosmith**; **Guns N' Roses**; **Stephen Hawking**; **Meat Loaf**; **Iron Maiden** (I know what you're thinking, but you should hear Stephen Hawking's guitar playing; he's like Yngwie Malmsteen)

Page 56: Some footballers from Euro 2000: **Karel Poborsky** (Czech Republic); **Zlatko Zahovic** (Slovenia); **Gheorghe Hagi** (Romania); **Savo Milosevic** (Yugoslavia); **Raul** (Spain); **Lilian Thuram** (France); **Alessandro Del Piero** (Italy); **Steve McManaman** (England); **Dennis Bergkamp** (Netherlands); **Abel Xavier** (Portugal); **Hakan Sükür** (Turkey); **Carsten Jancker** (Germany); **Erik Mykland** (Norway); **Freddie Ljungberg** (Sweden); **Peter Schmeichel** (Denmark); **Emile Lokonda Mpenza** (Belgium); **Edgar Davids** (Netherlands); **Luis Figo** (Portugal); **Luigi Di Biagio** (Italy); **Emmanuel Petit** (France)

Page 57: **Pierluigi Collina** (the best football referee in the world)

Page 58: **The Euro 2000 champions**: France

Page 59: **Liverpool FC squad 1999/2000** (why this particular season's squad, you may be wondering. Well, it was the first year of Minipops, so I just did the current. If I'd have waited a year, I'd have been able to do the treble winners. Wahey! Oh, and you may be wondering why there's not more footballers aside from this and the Euro 2000 stuff; well, I decided that to keep things calm, I'd not do any others. Although, by the time this book is on your bookshelf or in the cheap sale section of the book shop, there will be some Euro 2004 players on flipflopflyin.com, it's just that this book is being prepared before the tournament takes place, and dreams of England picking up the trophy are still bouncing like frisky sheep around my mind)

Page 60: **Busta Rhymes**; **Cameo**; **Phil Spector** (a truly remarkable producer and, seemingly, a not very good human being); **Hunter S Thompson**; **Kevin Rowland** (I used to work for a record distributor called 3mv and they distributed the releases of Creation Records when Kevin Rowland's dress-wearing comeback happened. There was a lot of stuff in the music press at the time which was taking the piss out of him, but beyond the stockings and suspenders, there was a really lovely album, which no one bought. It's a shame, but it does mean it's probably dead cheap in the bargain bins, and well worth 50p or something); **Tina Turner** (I can do a decent impression of her: should you ever meet me and I'm drunk enough, just ask, I might show you); **Simon and Garfunkel**; **Boney M**; **The Corrs**; **The Residents**

Page 61: **Che Guevara**; **Fidel Castro**; **Elian Gonzales** (a prime example of how, for a few weeks, someone can be amazingly famous. Thankfully for this fella, the fame didn't last long); **The Clinton family**, Bill, Hillary, and Chelsea; **Patty Hearst**; **Saddam Hussein**; **Margaret Thatcher**; **Adolf Hitler** (the last three are/were all nasty people. I would've done a George W Bush Minipop to make this evil trio into an evil quartet, but I just can't bring myself to look at his ugly, lying, cheating, war-mongering, hypocritical face for long enough); **the Dalai Lama** (after the storm of the previous few 'pops, a bit of serenity); **Napoleon Bonaparte**; **Abraham Lincoln**; **Tony Bloody Blair**

Page 62: **MC5**; **Spinal Tap**; **Black Sabbath**

Page 63: **Star Trek**; **Brian Potter** (*Phoenix Nights*); **Laurel & Hardy**; **Dame Edna Everage**; **Rolf Harris**; *The Young Ones*; *Trigger Happy TV*; *Scooby Doo*; *Mighty Morphin' Power Rangers*; *Seinfeld*; **Andy and Lou** (*Little Britain*); **Tommy Cooper**

Page 64: **Neil Young** (for a long time, I dismissed Neil Young as a whiny old fart whose guitar solos were too long. Now that I'm getting closer to the age of being an old fart, and indeed, starting to whine a bit about stuff in a way that will have me marked out by my future grandchildren as "a cantankerous old bugger", I'm starting to enjoy his music quite a lot)

Page 65: **Michael Jackson** × 3: Billie Jean; Black Or White; at the VMAs when he thought he'd won an award, but didn't.

Page 66: **Catatonia**; **Yeah Yeah Yeahs**; **The Velvet Underground and Nico**; **Can**; **Electric Six**; **The Shins**; **Franz Ferdinand**; **Phoenix** (who I saw play live recently, and it was one of the most enjoyable concerts I've been to. Not very interesting that fact, is it? But, y'know, if you ever get the chance to go and see them, you could do worse than to go along); **The Von Bondies**

Page 67: **Groove Armada**; **Stevie Wonder** (on the website, this one is animated. It kinda looks better like that); **Jimi Hendrix**; *Forrest Gump* (I enjoyed this film, then I read something somewhere that noted that the film is about an American citizen who achieves things by doing as he's told all the time; this has made me view it a little differently)

Page 68: **Machinehead**; **Amen**; **Monster Magnet**; **At The Drive-In**

Page 69: **Tindersticks**; **The Specials**; **The Cure**; **Dire Straits** (oooh, I ws a big big fan of Dire Straits when I was 15. I used to have posters literally all over my wall. There was a hi-fi shop in Lincoln and they had a bunch of these posters which were promotional things for Philips CD players. Anyway, the competition on said poster had passed its date and the chap in the shop let me have all of the posters. So I used them all. Every last one); **The Pogues**; **The Fall** (ah)

Page 70: **Walter Jabsco** the 2 Tone rude boy (2 Tone was the record label of The Specials, amongst others. This fellow was on the sleeve of their generic 7" sleeves)

Page 71: **Nick Cave**

Page 72: **Fugazi**; **Slade**; **Metallica**; **Supergrass**; **Mogwai**; **Depeche Mode**; **Sebadoh**; **Phish**; **Aqua**

Page 73: **Yasser Arafat and Ariel Sharon**: Minipops bringing you world peace!

Page 74: **Steps** x 2: Love's Got A Hold Of My Heart and Deeper Shade Of Blue; **Spice Girls**; **B*Witched**; **Lolly**; **All Saints**; **Daphne and Celeste**; **Scooch**; **Girl Thing**; **Hear'Say**; **Cheeky Girls**; **S Club 7** (This is, as I'm sure you've already worked out the girl group page, even though for me the words "girl group" conjure up thoughts of The Ronettes, The Shirelles, and The Shangri-Las. These girl groups, though, are from the end of the 20th century and predominantly British. Steps had two boys in the group, but were still far more girl than boy in style; Spice Girls you know about; B*Witched were Irish and contained the sisters of one of Boyzone; Lolly did a cover of the Toni Basil song, Mickey, bless her; All Saints' Never Ever was one of my favourite records of the Nineties; Daphne and Celeste were American and a bit mouthy; Scooch… err; pfff, all I can say is that a friend who worked at HMV once gave me a promotional Scooch lunch box which to this day contains screws and various IKEA screwdriver thingies; Girl Thing were touted as being the new Spice Girls and then failed to have hits quite dramatically; Hear'Say have a superfluous apostrophe and were winners of one of them TV shows; Cheeky Girls weren't winners of a TV thing, but they were twin sisters from Transylvania; S Club 7, finally, were four girls and three boys and made some splendid records)

Page 75: **Bros**; **Take That**; **A1**; **Westlife**; **Boyzone**; **Backstreet Boys**; **5ive**; **Point Break**; **Adam Rickitt**; **N Sync**; **3SL**; **Peter Andre**; **Blue with Elton John**; **Blue** on their own. (And this, as you'll also have probably noticed, is the boy band page. Bros came before all the others and wore Grolsch bottle tops on their shoes; Take That were the kings of boy bands; A1, err…; Westlife were/are about the most boring of all manufactured bands; Boyzone are the second most boring of all manufactured bands; Backstreet Boys… can't think of anything to say about them; 5ive spelt their name wrong; Point Break were insignificant; Adam Rickitt was an actor, then took his shirt off and became a singer; N Sync gave us Justin; 3SL, I think, but I'm not sure, contained the brothers of one of the women out of Steps; Peter Andre was a bit famous in the mid Nineties, and it seems has become famous again recently – the things that happen when you leave the country…; Blue's only real good thing was teaming up with Sir Elton for a version of one of his ace songs)

Page 76: **Victoria Beckham** (a footballer's wife); **Natalie Imbruglia**; **Vengaboys**; **No Doubt**; **Geri Halliwell**; **Dreem Teem**; **Deee-Lite** (I dunno if it's because of my age at the time, but the world seemed a better place when Groove Is In The Heart was on the radio a lot); **Masters At Work**; **Jamiroquai**

Page 77: **Britney Spears**; **Christina Aguilera**

Page 78: **Teenwolf**; *The Simpsons*; **Le Tigre**; **Pikachu**; *Singin' In The Rain* (my favourite film ever); **Jim Carrey in** *The Mask*; **Ali G**; **Ottowan**; **Pele**; **Uma Thurman in** *Kill Bill*

Page 79: **Pet Shop Boys** × 4: West End Girls (even though I have a feeling Chris never wore a cap in the video, he probably did at some point around then, so I'm sticking with it); Go West; Can You Forgive Her?; Nightlife

Page 80: **The Rutles**; **Jason Falkner** (used to be in Jellyfish; his solo records are exquisite); **Jellyfish**; **Beck** (in the Sexx Laws video); **Fun Boy Three**; **Guided By Voices**; **The Zombies**

Page 81: **Nirvana**

Page 82: **Outkast** (Hey Ya video); **MC Hammer**; **Nelly**; **Tupac**; **De La Soul**; **Rodney Jerkins**; **Dr Dre**; **Erykah Badu**; **NWA**; **NORE**; **So Solid Crew**

Page 83: **Nick Drake**; **Scritti Politti**; **Sinead O'Connor** (it's the Nothing Compares 2 U video); **Billy Ray Cyrus**; **The Jam**; **Ani DiFranco**; **DMX Krew**; **Dixie Chicks** (we love you); **XTC**; **Jewel**; **Henry Rollins**; **St Etienne**

Page 84: This is the German page: **Wir Sind Helden**; **Mia**; **Blumfeld**; **Die Ärzte**; **Lemonbabies**; **Rosenstolz**; **To Rococo Rot**; **Nena**; **Trio** (the first three are current indie-ish bands and are all rather good; Die Ärzte have been around for ages and one of their videos beat one I made at a film festival award ceremony recently, so I now hold a grudge; Rosenstolz are, ummm…; To Rococo Rot is a palindrome; Nena made more than just 99 Red Balloons; and Trio made more than just Da Da Da, and were exceedingly good too)

Page 85: **Kraftwerk** × 4: Die Mensch Maschine; Trans-Europe Express; The Mix; Expo 2000 (one thing I've noticed while writing these notes – and I've been doing them a bit at a time over a period of a fortnight so far – is that I've occasionally used this space to spout off about what I think is ace or rubbish. But, y'know, I've always wanted to do a book, and if that book allows me to talk about the pop groups I like or dislike, then all the better. With that in mind: I fucking love Kraftwerk)

Page 86: **Limp Bizkit**; **Korn**; **Bloodhound Gang**; **The Mission**; **Cheap Trick** (will always remind me of my old boss, Erik James, who was a man who used to sit at his desk air drumming. I'm sure that in his mind, he was always on stage with Cheap Trick. Or Rush); **The Clash**; **Linkin Park**; **Nickelback** (along with Busted, perhaps the worst thing ever to have toyed with my eardrums)

Page 87: **Tiger Woods**; **Mahatma Gandhi**; **William Shakespeare**; **Nusrat Fateh Ali Khan**

Page 88: **Jean Michel Jarre** (when I'm rich, I want one of those laser keyboards that I've tried to represent with this drawing); **Shania Twain**; **Robert Palmer**

Page 89: **Kurt Cobain** (in bad taste, I'm sorry); **Travis**; **Slint**; **Syd Barrett**; **The Beach Boys** (*Pet Sounds*); **Deep Purple** (*In Rock*); **Orbital** (live); **Red Hot Chili Peppers**

Page 90: **Harlem Globetrotters**; **The A-Team**; **The Monks**; **Evel Knievel**; **Jackson 5**; **Orgy**; *Ghostbusters*; **TLC**; *The Matrix*

Page 91: **Destiny's Child** (when there were four); **Beyoncé Knowles**; **Destiny's Child** (the globe-conquering three)

Page 92: **Rolling Stones** (this is the only Minipop of the Rolling Stones on the website version of Minipops. It's from the cover of the *Their Satanic Majesties Request* album. Rather a silly choice, I admit, that's why I rectified that on page 9 of this book); **Village People**; **The Jon Spencer Blues Explosion**; **Pink Floyd** (in *The Wall*)

Page 93: **Sleepy Jackson**; **Will Young**; **Carlos Santana**; **Phil Collins** (I know someone who's a big fan of Phil's. I never fail to take the piss, like the music snob I am); **DJ Hell**; **LCD Soundsystem**; **Lee "Scratch" Perry**; **Mr Acker Bilk**; **Craig David**; **Andrew WK**; **Robbie Williams**; **Woodchuck**; **Esquivel**; **Leo Sayer**; **Luke Slater**; **Momus**; **Tom Jones**; **Lenny Kravitz**; **Sisqo**; **Har Mar Superstar**

Page 94: **The Shangri-Las** (makers of some of the most dramatic, most beautiful music ever. See Leader Of The Pack, Past, Present And Future, and my favourite ever song, Remember (Walkin' In The Sand); **The Shaggs**; **The Bangles**; **Chicks On Speed**; **The Runaways**; **Kittie**; **Luscious Jackson**; **Las Ketchup**; **Cibo Matto**; **The Go-Go's**; **Misteeq**; **The Supremes**

Page 95: **Björk** × 4: Big Time Sensuality; It's Oh So Quiet; at Cannes, I think, for the premier of *Dancer In The Dark*; in *Dancer In The Dark*

Page 96: **Fatboy Slim** (or Norman Cook, depending on your naming preference); **Kylie** (mmmm…); **A-ha** (my sister's most favourite ever band); **The Wurzels**

Page 97: **Jesus Christ**

Page 98: **Crosby, Stills, Nash & Young**; **Evan Dando** (an odd choice of image. This was quite early in the Minipops' days. I think I found this image in an old copy of *The Face* magazine, where Evan Dando was in the woods with some nymph-ish models); **Queen** (car seat belts making good guitars for miming along to Brian May's solos with); **Pearl Jam**; **Red Hot Chili Peppers**; **Joy Division**; **Hanson**; **The Temptations**; **New York Dolls**

Page 99: **Showaddywaddy** (one of the first bands I ever saw live. I'm not sure which was the very first; it was either them, The Nolans, or The Spinners); **The Stone Roses** (there's a whole generation of people like me who'll get all misty-eyed if you say, "the end of I Am The Resurrection"); **Slipknot**; **2 Live Crew**

Page 100: **Boudicca**; **The Queen Mother**; **Queen Elizabeth I**; **Henry VIII**

Page 101: **The Hives**; **Ladytron**; **Echo & The Bunnymen**; **Boss Hog**; **Placebo**; **The Stranglers**; **Bush**; **Richie Hawtin**; **Elastica**; **Black Rebel Motorcycle Club**; **Jesus And Mary Chain**; **Suede** (as you will have noticed, all of these people are predominantly wearing black. I thought it might be kinda interesting to show how small differences can have a big impact on who the figure looks like)

Page 102: **Bob Dylan** × 2: Rolling Thunder Revue and Subterranean Homesick Blues; **Atomic Kitten** × 2: when they weren't so famous, and when they had some fame with a different third girl; **David Bowie** × 4: Ziggy Stardust; Thin White Duke; *Let's Dance*; *Earthling*

Page 103: **Elvis Costello**; **John Peel**; **Mariah Carey**; **Tom Waits**; **Nadia Comaneci**; **Fat Kid** off Fatboy Slim's *You've Come A Long Way*, Baby sleeve; **James Dean**; **Phillippe Starck**; **Missy Elliot** × 2 (can't remember which video the first picture is from, but the second is from the Work It video); **Carl Cox**; **Bob Marley**; **Gisele**; **Jesse Owens**; **Shakira** (I like Shakira. I like Shakira's music. Some of my friends may disown me for this); **DJ Shadow**; **Ian Thorpe** (the big-footed Australian swimmer); **John McEnroe**; **George Michael** × 2: (*Faith* and *Older* versions)

Page 104: **Tricky**; **Gareth Gates**; **PJ Harvey**; **Marvin Gaye**; **Gary Numan** (another one of those odd choices of reference points for a Minipop. This is how he looked during the *Beserker* era, which, I guess was at the point when his mainstream popularity started to tail off); **Buddy Holly**; **Eliza Carthy**; **Marilyn Manson**; **Rev. Al Sharpton**; **Elvis Presley**; **Carl Douglas** (the Kung Fu Fighting chap); **Xena**; **Underworld**; **Roky Erickson**; **John Lennon** and **Yoko Ono**; **Alvin Stardust**; **Billy Bragg**; **Mahir** (he was a bit of an internet star for a while, and is in the *Guinness Book Of Records* for the most visited personal homepage. His site is www.ikissyou.org); **Don King**; **Shaft**

Page 105: *Planet Of The Apes*: Cornelius; Dr Milo; Dr Zaius; Dr Zira; General Ursus; Taylor; Nova

Page 106: **Father Christmas**; **Snoop Doggy Dogg** (a Mizzle pizzle); **Muhammad Ali**; **Alanis Morissette** (possibly the most difficult surname to spell correctly without looking on Google)

Page 107: **Public Enemy** (somebody in the house say "yeah")

Page 108: **Bay City Rollers**; **Bucks Fizz**; **The Spinners**; **Throbbing Gristle**

Page 109: **Winston Churchill**; **Michael Eavis** (the bloke who lets his fields at Glastonbury be overrun by hippies every summer); **The Fonz**; **Stone Cold Steve Austin** (a wrestler)

Page 110: **Gomez**; **The Byrds**; **The Damned**; **Atari Teenage Riot**; **Pulp**; **Spiritualized**; **The Cramps**; **The Beach Boys** (*20/20*); **Blur**; **Captain Beefheart And His Magic Band**; **The Smiths**; **The Cardigans**

Page 111: **The Royal Tenenbaums**

Page 112: **Sting**; **Jan Hammer** (I was very very into *Miami Vice* when I was younger. I still am, really. I can't stop feeling that it's really cool. Thus, I also liked the theme tune and Crockett's Theme by Jan Hammer); **Moby**; **Avril Lavigne**; **Luciano Pavarotti**; **Miles Davis**; **Bruce Springsteen**; **David Crosby**; **Howard Stern**; **Yaphet Kotto** (a great actor who was in *Live And Let Die* and the brilliant TV series Homicide: Life On The Streets. He's depicted here as the character he played in Homicide, Lt. Al Giardello); **Mork and Mindy**; **Iggy Pop**

Page 113: **The Polyphonic Spree**

Page 114: **Rocky**; **Andy Kaufman** (coming to save the day); **Wonder Woman**; **Nicole Kidman**; **Marilyn Monroe**; **Bianca Jagger**; **Philip Marlow**; **James Bond**; **Ruth from *Six Feet Under***; **Jodie Foster**; **David Blaine** (levitating a bit); **The Osbournes**

Page 115: **Salvador Dalí**; **Jackson Pollock**; **Gilbert and George**; **Pablo Picasso**

Page 116: **Charlie Chaplin**; *The Wizard Of Oz* (sadly, I forgot to do Toto. Please imagine him there); *The Sound Of Music* (still makes me a bit doolally with happiness); *The King And I*; *Fight Club*; *O Brother, Where Art Thou?*; *The Big Lebowski*; **Jay and Silent Bob**; **Edward Scissorhands**; **Ace Ventura**; **Jacques Tati** (if you're ever in Brussels, then you need to go to the Atomium. Not only is it one of the best buildings in the whole wide world, they show Tati's film *Mon Oncle* there); **ET**; *Punch Drunk Love*; **Alfred Hitchcock**; **Freddy Krueger**; **Max Fischer** (*Rushmore*)

Page 117: **Bob Ross** (I thought for a long time about who should be on the very last page of the Minipops book, but I kept coming back to Bob Ross. He's been quite an influence on the look of the non-Minipops stuff I've done on Flip Flop Flyin'. He was a great man, and if I can be half as good as him, I'll be happy for ever more)

A few more notes:
1. I've not noted who everyone is because, well, I don't want to insult your intelligence and if you don't know who the person is, you all know how to use Google.
2. In the above text, I may have said something is the greatest/worst thing ever more than once. I can't help this over-exaggeration, it's something I do ALL the time.
3. I am from the UK, thus a lot of the references are British. I hope this doesn't spoil your enjoyment if you're from else-where in the world.

This book would not have happened, or wouldn't be the same, without these people. My heartfelt thanks to all of them: Hanni Pannier, Billy, Joanne Marie Robinson, Mum & Jim, Rüdiger & Karla Pannier, Becca Hardman, Ben Jones, Darren Betts, Delme Rosser, Derick & Jennifer Rhodes, Duncan Swain at radiotimes.com, Evyta & Reinout, Experimental Jetset, Hannah Barnes-Murphy, Helen Dobson, James Kendall, Jacqui Millar at Kinetic Foundation, John Bassett, Katy Thornton, Keith McColl, Marc Fernandez at Cashmere Games, Mark Hooper, Mother, Nina Kock, Patrick Burgoyne, Paula Carson, Steve McLay, Toke & Michael at K10k, and everyone who's suggested Minipops or wasted some of their employers' time at Flip Flop Flyin' over the past five years.